MARRIED AF

A funny MARRIAGE GUIDE for the Newlywed or Bride

WRITTEN BY Jen Marie Wiggins

ILLUSTRATED BY Jessica Smith

sourcebooks

Published by Sourcebooks
P.O. Box 4410, Naperville, Illinois 60567-4410
(630) 961-3900
sourcebooks.com

Printed and bound in the United States of America.
JOS 10 9 8 7 6 5 4 3 2 1

For my mom, who has always encouraged me to write and who still can't believe what AF means.

And for my husband, who is the best person I know. I am so grateful for "REAL" love stories.

Congrats IT'S HERE! YOU'RE TYING THE KNOT! A FEW WORDS FOR THE BRIDE ON WHAT MOM FORGOT...

LET'S BREAK
IT ALL DOWN
BEFORE THE
" I do,"
THE PARTS OF A
Marriage
SILLY, STRANGE, OR TABOO!

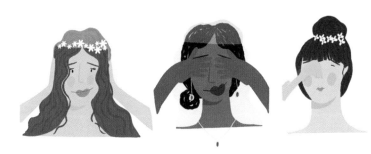

We'll start with your day.
This you should know!

For better or worse,
every bride's got to go.

The honeymoon's next,
and there, you're all set.
Though back in the day,
it wasn't all likes,
tweets, and texts.

In the newlywed phase,
you'll find it's a blast!
But buckle up, baby.
Some things don't last.

Get it?! Our PAPER anniversary...

With a spouse in the house,
your privacy's shot.

You'll never
again lay claim
to this spot.

And that goes for the bedroom.
The theory's the same.

Under the covers,
there'll be little shame.

But no need to stress.
Foreplay's not dead!

It's called shopping at Target...

or making the bed.

It may've started already.
You'll both see the change.

You go from selfies

to sleepy,

and grooming
gets strange.

One day, you're tweezing
while he's manscaping.

And you realize you're in it—
there's just no escaping.

There'll be fighting, of course—
things you wouldn't think:
a devotion to SportsCenter,
toenails in the sink.

There'll be ups.

There'll be downs.

Some days it's a dream.

Some days you're living
in a bad marriage meme.

Love's a beautiful mess—
such a gift and a ride!
And the best parts always
have nothing to hide.